SECOND THOUGHTS

NATIONAL
LIBRARY
OF AUSTRALIA

A catalogue record for this
book is available from the
National Library of Australia

Published 2022

ISBN: 978-0-6454300-9-7 (epub)
ISBN: 978-0-6455595-0-7 (paperback)
ISBN: 978-0-6455595-1-4 (hardcover)

`

9 780645 559507

Published with the aid of Jumble Publishing and Editing
(https://jumblepublishing.com)

Second thoughts

Joan Whitehead

ABOUT THE AUTHOR

Born and raised in the UK, Joan now lives in Western Australia, where she runs her own art and craft gallery and studio, creating and selling her own work.

She has always enjoyed creating things, from paintings and jewellery to glass work and books.

She is pleased to have had five books published in the past; the first one being a craft book, followed by four children's picture story books.

Another of her interests has always been writing rhymes and poems. She hopes you will find them interesting also.

CONTENTS

Waiting 2

Garden Magic 4

Fate 6

Sweet Song 8

The Scheme of Things 10

Snow 12

Jack Frost..14

The Fog 16

Love's Song 18

Dreaming 20

The Fire 22

Wonders 24

The Road 26

Nightmare..28

The Flat Mate 30

The Fight 32

Sayings 34

Smile..36

Patchwork Quilt 38

The Storm 40

The Day Has Begun 42

A Winter's Night 44

WAITING

He stands there
full of grace.

With a big smile
all over his face.

His eyes are black,
and his nose is red.

With a colourful scarf
and a hat on his head.

Waiting for his friends
to come out to play.

He waits in the sun
all through the day.

How long he stands
there we cannot say.

Soon Mr. Snowman
has melted away.

GARDEN MAGIC

The stars in
the sky sing
to the trees.

Apple blossom pink
and the
buzzing of the bees.

The garden is a
magical place.

It will put a smile
on anyone's face.

FATE

Fate is fickle so
they say

It shapes your
life in every way.

It makes you turn left
instead of right.

Or makes you run, when
you should fight.

6

Fate deals the cards
that you have to play.

It has a hand in
your life every day.

There's no use in trying
you have to give in.

Accept your fate,
put on a happy grin.

SWEET SONG

The little bird
sings as sweet as
can be,

way up high
in the lilac tree.

A song so sweet it
brings a tear to the eye

and makes you wish
that you could fly.

THE SCHEME
OF THINGS

In the vast
scheme of things,
who are we?

I am sure we can be
anything we want to be.

So move over there,
give me some room.

For I am a
flower about to bloom.

SNOW

The snow flake falls
onto the ground,

ever so gently
without any sound.

It looks so lovely
all crisp and white,

all sparkling and clean,
a beautiful sight.

A crisp white blanket
of deep cold snow,

through which only the
snowdrop will grow.

13

JACK FROST

Jack Frost waves his
bony hand,

a gripping cold
spreads over the land.

He turns the flowers and
the trees all white,

making everything
a beautiful sight.

THE FOG

The fog comes creeping
in the night,

taking everything with it
out of sight.

A blanket of mist
sweeps on by,

hiding the flowers
and trees from the eye.

LOVE'S SONG

Sing a song,
a song of love.

The sun and the moon
and the stars above.

To sing a song so
sweet and so true.

With a heart full of
love just for you.

To walk down a rainbow
with love hand in hand.

To run in the meadow
and over the land.

My love has no bounds
as it flows out of me.

As high as the sky,
as deep as the sea.

DREAMING

A Dream is like a song,
a beautiful refrain.

Drifting along on the
astral plane.

We can go anywhere
as we lie there in bed.

Any flight of fancy
that comes into our head.

To soar on high like
a bird in flight.

A star or moonbeam,
a shaft of light.

Then like a candle in the wind,
a small flickering flame.

Our dreams are over,
it's back to reality again.

THE FIRE

A lightning strike,
or a careless flame.

Who is at fault,
who is to blame?

A tiny spark that goes
on and on.

Soon all greenery is
dead and gone.

The fire knows no
bounds as it flows on by.

It's so sad, it brings
a tear to the eye.

But nature lends a hand,
down comes the rain.

The fire is over,
flowers bloom again.

WONDERS

The blades of grass sing
in the breeze,

as the wind flows
on by,

down to the valley
and up to the sky,

spreading earth's seeds
far and wide.

My thoughts are like
seeds ready to grow.

Flowers of every colour
wait in my dreams.

Deep in the forest
where no man has been.

I ponder at
wonders there to be seen.

THE ROAD

The road stretches on
as far as you can see.

As high as the mountains,
as far as the sea.

Come this way it seems
to say.

Over the hill and
far away.

Through pastures green,
yellow and blue.

They sing in the sun
and beckon to you.

Stay in the meadow, bask
in the sun.

But the road is there,
it goes on and on.

NIGHTMARE

A nightmare is a thing
that you do dread.

Even though you know
it's all in your head.

They can give you
an awful fright.

Wake you up in
the middle of the night.

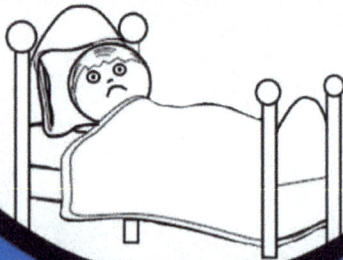

You lie there in bed
as the hours fly by.

You can't get to sleep
no matter how hard you try.

Finally you nod off and
drift into a dream.

The nightmare is over,
or so it would seem.

THE FLAT MATE

All day I wait to hear
her key in the door.
To see her face makes
my heart soar.

But it will be "Hello, Harry,
have you had a nice day?"
Then not even stopping
to hear what I say.

Off to the bedroom to
get ready for her date.
Heaven help, that her new
him should have to wait.

Why can't it be like
it used to be.
When it was just her
and little old me.

Playing together and
sitting in the sun
She would tell me her secrets
she never told anyone.

But I'm just good old Harry
her flat mate.
Can't she see how I love her.
Is it to late?

Oh, there's a knock on the door
it must be her new beau.
Off out without me,
I wonder where they will go.

Somewhere that she
couldn't take me.
As I am an Old English
Sheepdog, you see.

THE FIGHT

Tempers frayed,
voices raised.
Fists shook
eyes blazed.

Coats came off
and with no more ado,
the fight was on
and punches flew.

A crowd gathered
round to see the sight.
Everyone likes to
see a good fight.

Down went one,
with a blow to the head,
falling down like a lump
of lead.

32

They all thought the
fight was done
but a hush fell on the crowd —
in his hand, there was a gun.

A shot rang out,
there was a splash of red —
and everyone knew one
of them was dead.

The crowd faded away,
they had had their fun.
One lay dead,
the other a fugitive on the run.

A heated argument
is all that it takes.
One thoughtless second
and many lives it breaks.

SAYINGS

Lightning never strikes in the same place twice, they say.

The grass is always greener on the other side of the hill far away.

A new broom always sweeps clean, so sweep on,

and remember two heads are better than one.

A friend in need is a friend indeed, that's true.

You can't have your cake and eat it too.

A bird in the hand is
better than in the bush, you see.

You can't throw stones in glass
houses, you will agree.

A rolling stone gathers
no moss, so they say.

If you run away you
can fight another day.

A stitch in time
does really save nine.

So follow these sayings
and you will be fine.

SMILE

A smile is as infectious
as a plague can be.

Smile at anyone you meet.
it will catch on, you see.

Soon it will spread
all over the land.

Make you feel happy,
make you feel grand.

It will put an end to
lots that are sad.

A smile lifts you up,
makes you feel glad.

To work its magic
could take many days.

But work it will
in lots of ways.

Over the hills and
sea it could flow.

Round the world and back
to you, it could go.

So smile at everyone
start a new trend.

Goodness knows where
that smile will end.

PATCHWORK QUILT

Squares of cloth cut out
with great care.

All the pieces
lying there.

Some squares are plain
some are spotted

some are striped
some are dotted

Red and yellows,
greens and blues.

Every colour that
you can use.

All the squares are very gay.

A rainbow of colours in every way.

Together they make a colourful show.

The work is a joy watching it grow.

Sewn together with needle and thread.

Making a delightful quilt for the bed.

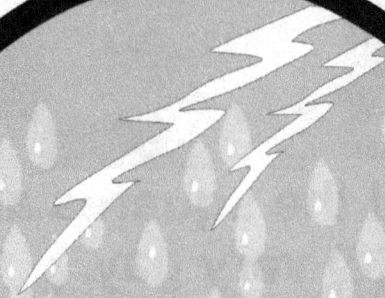

THE STORM

Lightning flashes
thunder roars.

Rain falls down
it simply pours.

The storm has passed
by, its course is run.

Everything sparkles
and shines in the sun.

THE DAY HAS BEGUN

The morning dew
clings to the trees.

Sparkling and shining
in the breeze.

The butterfly flies
up to the sun.

Telling the world
that the day has begun.

Cotton wool clouds
drift lazily by,

high up above,
in the clear blue sky.

The fluttering birds
fly to and fro.

Up in the trees
and down below.

Is it spring at last,
they all seem to say.

All winter long,
waiting for this day.

Spring bursts forth
chasing those blues away.

But is the nice weather
here to stay?

A WINTER'S NIGHT

Things to do on a
cold winter's night.

Close the curtains
and put on the light.

Shut out the world,
so no one can see.

Stoke up the fire, get
it as warm as can be.

Holding hands, we
can just sit and chat.

Some people wouldn't
think a lot of that.

Listen to some music,
soft and low.

Or whisper things
you want to know.

Simple things can
bring the most pleasure.

Looking back, it's
these we most treasure.

Sharing ones life with
the one that you love.

It's like the sun, the moon
and the stars above.

<u>Also by Joan Whitehead</u>

Step by step Transparent Art

Not Green

The Four Seasons of Sammy Snail

Flowery Thoughts

Piggy Tales*

Ten Ways to Please Your Mum*

* Coming soon

www.ingramcontent.com/pod-product-compliance
Lightning Source LLC
Chambersburg PA
CBHW071435040426
42445CB00012BA/1373